FREEMIUM

Attract more customers and boost your sales

Written by Mouna Guidiri
In collaboration with Anne-Christine Cadiat
Translated by Carly Probert

FREEMIUM

KEY INFORMATION

- **Names:** Freemium, crippleware.
- **Uses:** Business model, adapted for digital products and digital data.
- **Why is it successful?** Original cost management, massive attraction of customers, adapted to digital products.
- **Key words:** Freemium, free, premium, digital, conversion rate.

INTRODUCTION

There's No Such Thing as a Free Lunch. This title of a book by the American economist Milton Friedman (1912-2006) speaks volumes about the attitude of the majority of economists towards free items: they simply do not exist.

> ### GOOD TO KNOW: *THERE'S NO SUCH THING AS A FREE LUNCH*
>
> This phrase, from an unknown author, was popularised by economists such as Friedman. It refers to the illusion of free offers: everything has a price, whether direct or indirect, visible or hidden.

However, a quick browse of the applications offered on the internet provides several counter-examples, including

Spotify, Dropbox and antivirus software. Nonetheless, these products are not completely free:

- Spotify limits free listening time;
- Dropbox only offers some storage space for free;
- the antivirus software only offers reduced protection.

These applications have the same mode of distribution: the offer includes a free version and a more sophisticated or fully developed paid version (premium).

History

The distribution of free samples has already existed for a long time. Offering a small amount of a product (food, shampoo, drinks, etc.) is a tried and tested practice, because it can attract customers and subtly encourage them to purchase the product. This practice has inspired the freemium model, which works in a similar way in a virtual environment. This type of free offer is a business model (a model summarising the activities of a business: objectives, processes and resources used) first developed in the 1980s, especially for software. In 2006, Jarid Lukin from the company Alacra gave it the name 'freemium', a combination of 'free' and 'premium'.

Definition of the model

The freemium model is a business model that combines two pricing strategies. For the same product, the model offers two versions: one is free and allows unrestricted access, the other is paid-for and offers from improved or additional services.

The strategy behind this model is based on the possibility that the free version will attract a large number of users and, above all, make them loyal customers. The aim is to convert as many users of the free version as possible into users of the paid version.

This model cannot be used for any product. Although several cases illustrate its suitability for software or video games, it is challenging for cultural products in particular. This is therefore a strategy with the potential for significant added value, but it requires careful analysis of the context of the product, the services attached to it, as well as any operating costs, distribution costs, etc. beforehand.

THEORY

WHAT KIND OF FREE?

There are different types of free offers:

- **A free offer to attract customers and encourage them to buy the product.** This type is based on the sale of complementary products alongside the free basic product (for example, a free razor with the purchase of three blades).
- **A free offer supported by a third party/intermediary.** This type depends on advertisers who finance the producer in exchange for advertising space, knowing that the advertiser is in turn funded by the consumer indirectly (the relative price of advertising is integrated into the product price covered by the advertiser).
- **A free offer in exchange for reputation.** This is the least common type in a market economy: the free offer is given in exchange for attention, reputation, etc., which have no monetary value.

Types of free offers

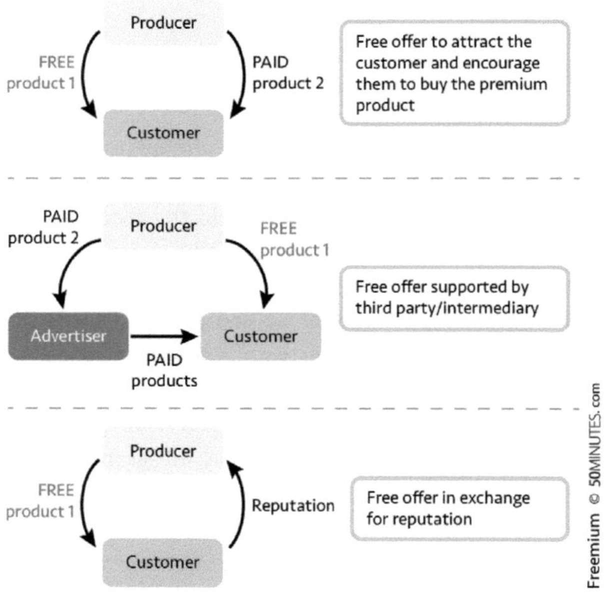

- **Freemium** is a business model that exploits free items in such a way that a small share of consumers pay for the entire community of users to enjoy the free offer.

Freemium

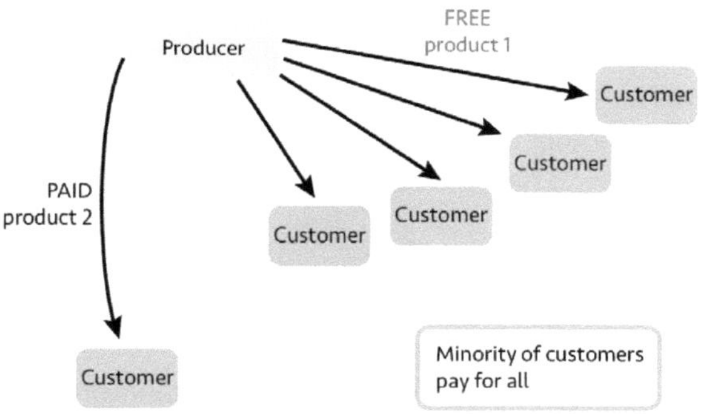

The venture capitalist Fred Wilson encourages the use of freemium and makes his views clear on his blog: "Give your service away for free, possibly ad supported but maybe not, acquire a lot of customers very efficiently through word of mouth, referral networks, organic search marketing, etc., then offer premium priced value added services or an enhanced version of your service to your customer base."

<u>**GOOD TO KNOW: VENTURE CAPITALIST**</u>

A venture capitalist is someone invests in young companies or startups characterised by high financial risk as well as strong growth potential.

BETWEEN FREE AND PREMIUM

The balance of freemium is therefore based on a mixed offer, with free and paid versions of the same product.

This is not a socialist model, where the ultimate goal is to provide the products in question to a particular segment of the customer base for free. Companies that opt for this business plan are constantly hoping to acquire new customers who are willing to pay for the premium version.

How is this free offer model financed? How does it attract premium customers? To answer these questions, it is important to highlight that freemium is particularly suitable for digital products or those relating to information technology, which are therefore largely linked to the use of computers and the internet. Given that the cost of acquiring and using computers and the internet is decreasing, the development of products for this type of media is becoming less and less expensive. This reduction in production costs can be illustrated by the example of MP3 files: it costs only a negligible amount more to create 100 or even 10 000 copies than to produce the first version. In economic terms, the marginal cost (the cost generated by the second unit produced) in this situation is close to zero. Thus, the sale of a defined number of products is enough to cover all the production costs. This new reality has made a major contribution to the development of freemium in the digital domain. Furthermore, it is now possible to set usage limits in terms of time or functionality on digital products and services.

Since the free distribution of a certain number of their products does not lead to high costs, companies whose products are suitable apply this model to attract as many customers as possible. While customers' interest in the free version is closely linked to the lack of transaction costs, the profitability of this type of model is based on the percentage of users – initially attracted to the free product – who will decide to pay for the premium version. This percentage is called the 'premium conversion rate'. As it is obvious that no rational person would pay for a product that they could get for free, it is important to ensure that the free and premium formulas are different by adding significant extra value to the second version and making it compelling enough for the customers who are willing to pay.

TYPES OF PREMIUM

This added value can take various forms, which are grouped into different categories of premium:

- **The first category offers additional options.** In the free version, basic services are offered. The paid version offers improved versions of the same services, or possibly additional advanced services. Skype is the best example of this: consumers can make PC to PC calls for free, but they pay for calls to mobile phones. The challenge is therefore for the basic services to push basic users towards the more sophisticated version.
- **The second category offers free services, but for a limited time.** There are two different options:
  - The first allows limited periods of use. For example, Spotify initially offered 10 hours of free listening time per month (although it has since lifted this time limit), with unlimited listening in the paid version (streaming).
  - The second is more suitable for software. For example, users can access a trial version of the Microsoft Office suite. It is complete, including all services, but there is a time limit – access is subsequently blocked permanently unless the full version of the software has been purchased. In this scenario, the purchase is motivated by the habit of using the product, which leads the customer to acquire the permanently accessible version.
- **The third category involves limitations in terms of quantity.** There is usually a limited number of free megabytes (MB) or gigabytes (GB), which measure the

storage space offered by the producer for this type of product or service. For instance, Dropbox offers a fixed amount of free storage, but anything above that requires payment.

- **The last category is linked to the number of users who benefit from the product.** Only one user can use the service for free. To add another user on the same computer, they must pay a set price. The HipChat service illustrates this type of freemium. The site allows the first five users to enjoy the full offer (group chat, which is often used in the workplace) for free, but as soon as a sixth person registers, the free offer expires and each user (even the first five) pays a flat fee per month.

The first category presents a kind of freemium based on different options, while the last three are more focused on capacity. Although this categorisation outlines the most common types of freemium, it is of course not exhaustive.

In the following section, we will explain the challenges faced by entrepreneurs who opt for the freemium model.

LIMITATIONS AND EXTENSIONS

Freemium is a model that carries risks. On the one hand, it offers significant advantages in terms of customer attraction and an original way of managing production costs. On the other hand, it remains a difficult model to implement as it entails several risks that can be limiting when the model is poorly suited to the product.

LIMITATIONS AND CRITICISMS

Beware of freeloaders!

Freeloaders – who are only attracted to the product because it is free – are the greatest risk, since the premium offer is never attractive enough in their eyes. If, in the worst-case scenario, all users prove to be freeloaders (meaning a conversion rate of 0), the freemium model will be a complete failure.

The result could be the same if the consumers, who are not freeloaders to begin with, are not attracted by the advantages of the paid version.

Competition

Competition – which is not new – can also be a significant danger. Freemium offers on similar products will inevitably offer substitute services. This situation risks creating a significant loophole, as users can juggle and switch from one brand to another to enjoy the free offers, continuously benefiting from trial premium versions without paying.

Problems for the customer

Alongside these risks to the entrepreneur, there are also some disadvantages for consumers. In particular, the customer has limited control over the free product. The user's ability to make demands is actually very limited. In other words, whereas the customer is in control under normal circumstances, this privilege is cancelled when the product they are using is free. For example, an application used for free on the internet can disappear overnight without notice, which will probably cause problems for customers who are used to this offer.

Furthermore, a particular case of freemium is highly controversial: the principle of pay-to-win in video games. In this case, players who subscribe to the premium version increase their chances of winning, regardless of their talent.

RELATED MODELS AND EXTENSIONS

Financing from advertising

Adware is one of the extensions of freemium. These are services offered for free but with permanent and sometimes very distracting advertising. This advertising can cover the costs of software or video game development while preserving it as a free offer. However, it is possible to obtain an ad-free version by paying. As such, adware can be classed as a type of freemium if we consider that the premium version is the version without advertising.

Freeware

Freeware (a combination of 'free' and 'software') is software that can be used for free, but with usage limits. The free version can be used as a loss leader to encourage users to purchase the paid version or other products by the same developer. The aim may also be to create an addictive effect: by offering the product for free, it becomes a standard in the field. This technique may rely on a trial period: the product is only free for a limited time.

Freemium for culture

When these limits are well analysed and, above all, used as indicators of adaptability – or lack thereof – of the freemium version of the product, this model retains its potential profitability.

Its relevance is proven by the extension that is made by some industries, particularly those related to culture. For example, in the music industry marginal costs are very low, thanks to the invention of CDs and, later, the MP3. Furthermore, some artists, such as Radiohead in 2007 and Nine Inch Nails in 2008, adopted freemium and turned it into a commercial strength: they chose to offset the free download of their album by increasing the price of concert tickets or selling exclusive versions of their album.

PRACTICAL APPLICATION

THE GOLDEN RULES OF FREEMIUM: SUCCESS FACTORS

In practice, for a freemium business model to succeed, entrepreneurs must respect a number of points which should be considered before judging the product's suitability.

These success factors can be summarised in four steps.

- Firstly, success involves reaching the target and potential prospects: the freemium mechanism is closely related to the number of consumers of the free version. Indeed, the more people are interested in using the basic version for free, the better the chance of gaining real customers who are willing to pay to upgrade to the more sophisticated version.

Success factor: The target audience should be broad. Since the percentage of customers opting for the paid version is generally low, it is useful to expand the customer base of free users so that the number of premium conversions is high enough to cover the production costs. This requires good product visibility and an emphasis on the free aspect.

- Next, it is important to ensure good quality: we have already discussed of the customer's limited ability to make demands, justified by the fact that the product is free, but this observation must be qualified: if producers want to attract customers and encourage them to purchase the premium version, they must offer free versions with options (not too few) that provide a real taste of the paid version. Like perfume samples that are distributed for free to attract new customers, the free offer must accurately represent the premium offer. The illusion of premium, created by the free version, will then be strengthened through word of mouth and networks, which play a fundamental role in terms of communication. This reality is double-edged, as criticisms of the product's quality can also circulate quickly and have a greater influence than in the case of a normal product. The influence of opinion leaders results in a decrease or increase in the number of free users, as well as the number of consumers of the premium version.

Success factor: Freemium should be considered as a model that allows the customer to test the product before buying it. The mission is to satisfy the customer in terms of quality and win them over to the product or service.

- It would also be wise to minimise the operation costs of the free version. This minimisation aims to reduce the number of premium users needed to cover the production and marketing costs of both versions. This approach is directly related to the marginal cost of production, which should be as close to zero as possible. In other words, the duplication of the product in its free and paid versions must be achieved at minimal cost. It is also recommended to apply the same reasoning with regards to distribution: the transfer much be reasonably cheap, fast and without restrictions. The key to success is financing the production of both versions of the product through the subscription fees paid by premium customers. We have already seen that, in the case of digital data, applying the freemium model does not pose a problem since it is easy to control marginal costs and distribution. However, these elements can present a major obstacle if this business model is applied to a material product.

Success factor: As with the first step, the trick is finding the financial balance, although this time the focus is more on the offer. Whereas the first step aims to maximise potential buyers, this step seeks to minimise potential costs.

- The last step is to encourage transition to the premium offer: this is the greatest challenge of the freemium model. If all the previous steps are followed, the free version will be able to capture the attention of as many users as possible. As we explained in the first step, this maximisation will later have an impact on the number of premium customers. However, the initial situation (many free users, but few premium customers) risks holding back development if the successful features of the free version reduce interest in the premium version. It is therefore essential to choose the right type of freemium and the right complementary services to include only in the paid version. The benefits of moving to premium must be clear to see and easy to evaluate.

Success factor: The conversion rate is the main interest at this stage. This rate, along with the operating costs of the model, determines the success or failure of the freemium model. A high conversion rate is achieved by making users of the free version loyal to the product or service and adopting an effective strategy, whether this concerns the benefits of the premium version or the clarity and visibility of information about these advantages.

> "If the trial satisfies the customers and the premium offer appeals to them even more, the challenge is won and the balance is maintained."

CASE STUDIES: SKYPE AND SPOTIFY

Skype

Skype was created in 2003 by Janus Friis (born in 1976) and Niklas Zennström (born in 1966) as a new free means of instant written (IM: Instant Messaging) and oral (VoIP: Voice over IP) communication. Later on, the option of video calls was introduced. Skype was bought by eBay in 2006, then by Microsoft in 2011.

Alongside its offer of free services, this innovative concept offers paid premium services, in particular SkypeOut, which allows calls to landlines and mobile phones. Although it is not free, this service remains competitive with regards to standard telephone communications, especially for long distance calls. Furthermore, it is also possible to purchase a Skype number to receive calls from landlines and mobile phones. This is called SkypeIn.

At first glance, there are many potential Skype users. The possibility of using a computer, the savings in communication costs and the good call quality attract customers and encourage them to adopt this revolutionary application. In addition to the quality of service, the network effect also plays an important role and subtly attracts potential customers: the features made available by the free version of Skype are useless if the user's friends do not have a Skype account. In concrete terms, it is difficult to convert to a pro-gramme if the user must convince their entire contact list to do the same. As for the attractiveness of the premium version, this stems firstly from the loyalty described above, and secondly from the price competitiveness compared with standard telephone offers.

By 2014, an average of 184 million people used Skype each month. Of these, 8.1 million had subscribed to one of the two premium packages available. With a conversion rate of over 6% and technology that evolves at the same pace as the users' computers, the profitability of the application is guaranteed.

In addition, the operating costs are minimised. For example, in 2010, only 65 of the company's 839 employees worked in customer service, as customer service has been partially replaced by discussion and support forums between users.

However, there are some risks: the competition that Skype represents for telephone operators could lead them to cancel their various partnerships and block the possibility of SkypeIn and SkypeOut, denying Skype access to their networks, for example.

Moreover, the relatively recent acquisition of Skype by Microsoft makes it difficult to predict how the business model of this revolutionary means of communication will develop. There is even the possibility that it could turn into an entirely paid-for service What is certain is that the VoIP market promises plenty of action over the next decade and that many paths of development must be taken into account.

In summary, the example of Skype illustrates all the steps to follow and the criteria for making freemium a success, although there are still risks of deviation. These may include risks related to the cost structure (cancellation of partnerships with telephone operators) and threats to users (transition to a paid model for all services).

Spotify

Spotify is an interesting freemium case study as it allows us to highlight the new wave of applications that allow free online music streaming.

Spotify was created in 2006 by two Swedish entrepreneurs, Daniel Ek (born in 1983) and Martin Lorentzon (born in 1969). The main service offered by the application is the streaming (an alternative to downloading) of music online. This service was initially available in three forms:

- The most basic form was Spotify Open, which allowed free online music listening. However, this listening was regularly interrupted by advertisements.
- The second option was Spotify Unlimited, which eliminated advertising breaks with the monthly payment of a set amount.

- The third option, Spotify Premium, was the most expensive and most advanced. It complemented the first two by allowing listeners to use the same account on a tablet or smartphone, even without internet connection.

At present, users can choose between Spotify Free, which more or less corresponds to Spotify Open, Spotify Premium, which offers the same service but without advertisements and with the option of listening offline, and Spotify Family, which offers premium features for up to five people.

To attract and create a good customer base for the free version, Spotify did not directly benefit from a network effect, as in the case of Skype. Two techniques were used to fill this gap:

1. **Collaboration with social networks like Twitter and Facebook.** This strategy gave Spotify users the opportunity to share songs on these networks. Since the music shared in this way cannot be listened to without installing Spotify and creating an account, this led to a rapid increase in the number of users.
2. **A registration strategy by invitation only (during the launch phase).** As these invitations were limited, users who wanted to share their music listening experience had to choose from their contacts and invite only those who were most likely to appreciate Spotify's services at their fair value. In this way, from its launch Spotify had a significant number of potential premium customers.

In 2016, Spotify reached over 100 million active monthly

users, around 30% of whom were paying for the service.

The biggest obstacle faced by the company is the obligation to purchase the necessary licenses to distribute music from the production companies and labels involved. Indeed, this generates the majority of costs, since the streaming itself is not expensive (the programme is installed on the user's computer, as with Skype). This represents a threat regarding the condition relating to near-zero marginal costs, which is central to the freemium model.

With regards to the evolution of the Spotify model, there have already been some significant changes. For example, restrictions on listening in the free version (no more than ten hours of free listening per month and a maximum of five plays per song) were introduced and later lifted, and the range of options offered has changed since the programme's launch.

Do these changes reflect a desire to move to a more standard business model where all services are paid-for? This could be the case, given the size of the user base already established, which could be considered sufficient for a conversion to an all-paying model.

Ultimately, Spotify is characterised by the originality of the combination of several business models: funding from subscriptions, but also through advertising, the exploitation of advertising to make the premium version more attractive, etc. In addition, in the long term, the possibility of adopting a system where only a premium account would be available cannot be ruled out, because the dependence on record labels makes the business's cost structure more complex.

SUMMARY

- Several types of free offers exist in the market economy. Freemium is one of these offers. It involves offering two versions of a product or service: a free version and a paid-for (premium) version.
- The advantages of the paid version generally involve access to improved or additional services compared with the free version.
- Firstly, the aim of the strategy is to attract the as many customers as possible.
- Secondly, the objective is to maximise the conversion rate, which refers to the percentage of users of the free version who convert to the premium version.
- There are several categories of freemium: the premium version may provide additional options (Skype), the ability to use the service without limits or restriction (Spotify), or the possibility for multiple users to access to the same product (HipChat).
- Freemium is not a suitable business model for all products: the risks of freeloaders or increased competition may outweigh its added value.
- The disadvantage for the user is the limited control they have over the free version.

We want to hear from you!
Leave a comment on your online library
and share your favourite books on social media!

FURTHER READING

BIBLIOGRAPHY

- Anderson, C. (2009) *Free: The Future of a Radical Price.* London: Pearson.
- Beecroft, N. (2013) Demystifying the Freemium Model. *Binkd.* [Online]. [Accessed 14 May 2014]. Available from: <http://binkd.com/marketing/demystifying-the-freemium-model/>
- Bomsel, O. (2010) *L'économie immatérielle : industries et marchés d'expériences.* Paris: Gallimard.
- Compare Business Products (2011) *The Best and Worst Uses of the Freemium Business Model.* [Online]. [Accessed 14 May 2014]. Available from: <http://www.comparebusinessproducts.com/fyi/best-worst-freemium-businesses>
- Freemium model website: http://www.freemium.org/
- Murgia, M. (2016) Spotify crosses 100m users. *The Telegraph.* [Online]. [Accessed 8 February 2017]. Available from: <http://www.telegraph.co.uk/technology/2016/06/20/spotify-crosses-100m-users/>
- Porter, M. E. (2001) Strategy and the Internet. *Harvard Business Review.* [March edition].
- Rosoff, M. (2010) Spotify Bleeding from Licensing Costs. *Business Insider.* [Accessed 14 May 2014]. Available from: <http://www.businessinsider.com/spotify-needs-more-paying-subscribers-to-survive-2010-11>
- Skype website: http://www.skype.com/

- Spotify website:
  http://www.spotify.com/
- Wiels, J. (2012) Le Freemium, nouvelle recette ou vieille formule ? *Regards sur le numérique.* [Online]. [Accessed 14 May 2014]. Available from: <http://www.rslnmag.fr/post/2012/03/26/Le-freemium-nouvelle-formule-ou-vieille-recette-.aspx>
- Wilson, F. (2006) My Favorite Business Model. *AVC (blog).* [Online]. [Accessed 14 May 2014]. Available from: <http://www.avc.com/a_vc/2006/03/my_favorite_bus.html>

IMPROVE YOUR GENERAL KNOWLEDGE

IN A BLINK OF AN EYE !

www.50minutes.com